OGIER, Susan

A sense of
place

STEP-UP
ART AND DESIGN

A Sense of Place

Susan Ogier

Evans

Published by Evans Brothers Limited
2A Portman Mansions
Chiltern Street
London W1U 6NR

© Evans Brothers Limited 2009

Produced for Evans Brothers Limited by
White-Thomson Publishing Ltd,
Bridgewater Business Centre,
210 High Street,
Lewes, East Sussex BN7 2NS

Printed in Hong Kong by New Era Printing Co. Ltd

Project manager: Rachel Minay

Designer: Leishman Design

British Library Cataloguing in Publication Data

Ogier, Susan

    A Sense of Place – (Step-up Art & Design)

    1. Art and design – Juvenile literature

    I. Title

    372.5'2

ISBN 978 0237 535 797

Acknowledgements:

Special thanks to Mrs Pat Allen and the teachers and pupils in Years 3, 4, 5 and 6 at St Luke's Primary School, Kingston upon Thames, Surrey, for all their artwork and help in the preparation of this book.

Picture acknowledgements:

BrandX Pictures: pages 4b, 16; Bridgeman Art Library: pages 6b (Private Collection), 15l (Private Collection, © The Maas Gallery, London, UK), 15r (Phoenix Art Museum, Arizona, USA, Louis Cates Memorial Fund), 20l (Kunsthistorisches Museum, Vienna, Austria), 20r (Pushkin Museum, Russia); Corbis: pages 8t (Fine Art Photographic Library), 8b (National Gallery Collection; By kind permission of the Trustees of the National Gallery, London), 13t (Michael & Patricia Fogden), 19t (Stapleton Collection), 21 (Philadelphia Museum of Art), 26b (Richard A. Cooke); Chris Fairclough: cover (main), pages 6t, 7, 9 (all), 17 (all), 19b, 22b, 25, 29; Edward Hopper: page 23; Istockphoto: pages 5t&b, 10t, 14t&b, 28; Kobal Collection: page 22t (20th [Century] Fox); Shutterstock: cover tl&r, title page, [pages] 10b, 11 (all), 12 (all), 14c, 15t&b, 24 (all), 27; St Luke's Primary School, [Kingston] upon Thames: page 13b.

Contents

The local environment

Getting to know the area where we live and grow up helps us to develop our 'sense of place'. What are the main features of your local area? Buildings? Green spaces? Traffic? People? What can you smell? What sounds do you hear?

▶ *Do you live in a rural or an urban area? What do you like about your area? Is there anything about it you would like to be different?*

Wish you were here...

Imagine you are a travel agent. Write and illustrate a brochure to persuade day-trippers or holidaymakers to come to your area. Think about all the good things you know about your neighbourhood, and try to discover new information by visiting your local museum or library.

Use your memory

How often do you really look at the things you pass every day? Close your eyes and try to visualise your journey from home to school. Are there particular features that you can remember? Draw them from memory in your sketchbook.

Use your senses

Our five senses can help to tell us about our surroundings. Not only what we can see and hear around us, but smells, tastes and textures all help to give us a sense of place.

Sensory journal

Make a journal, based on the five senses, of your local area. Begin by stapling or stitching small/A5 pages together to make a paper book. Then stick in items that represent a sensory journey around your area.

• 'Sight' could mean sketches of local buildings or people. A river could be shown by silver foil.

• For 'touch', you could include textured paper, such as wallpaper to represent your home or sandpaper to represent roads, or rubbings of brickwork or tree bark.

• For 'taste' and 'smell', you could take photos of restaurants or food shops, copy local recipes, or glue down scattered spices or coffee grains.

• 'Sound' could mean found objects such as dead leaves or gravel, or be shown by pictures of traffic or a railway.

Celebrate your area

In your classroom, make a display of your local area with the sensory journals and your brochures. Perhaps you could celebrate the different cultures that exist in your area by bringing in special foods for everyone to try.

The smooth ramps at the skatepark are great for doing tricks on my skateboard.

My sister and I love the local park – we can hear birdsong, children laughing and aeroplanes overhead.

Sketching the environment

A sketch is a way of taking notes by drawing instead of writing. Some artists like to think in pictures rather than words, and a quick and easy way for them to jot down ideas or interesting scenes is to make thumbnail sketches.

What is a thumbnail sketch?

The word 'thumbnail' gives a clue about the small size of these sketches. Just as we might make short notes to remind us about something, thumbnail sketches allow an artist to make small, quick visual notes that can be used later on.

JMW Turner

JMW Turner was one of Britain's most popular landscape artists. Turner used hundreds of sketchbooks in his lifetime, in which he recorded the scenes he saw while travelling.

Turner at the Tate

Browse through Turner's sketchbooks online at:
http://www.tate.org.uk/britain/turner/

▲ Look closely at these thumbnail sketches. Can you see the type of marks that the artist has used in order to record the features she noticed in the environment?

▲ This is one of Turner's watercolour sketches. Turner was interested in showing the effects of light and atmosphere in his work and his techniques were considered revolutionary at the time.

Using a viewfinder

Draw some small rectangles on a page in your sketchbook. You are going to fill these with thumbnail sketches of your local environment.

Use a viewfinder to help you to focus on one small area in a scene. This will make it easier for you to choose exactly what to sketch.

Make a flexible viewfinder by cutting two 'L' shapes from a piece of paper or card and place them so that they create a space in the middle. Try sliding the two together and apart again to make different sized rectangles for you to look through.

I can make the aperture larger or smaller with this viewfinder, so that I can choose whether I want more or less in my scene.

Quick on the draw

Working very fast, without worrying about mistakes, is an important part of making thumbnail sketches. The artist can collect a lot of information quickly by just drawing the main shapes, lines, or areas of dark and light in a scene.

How quickly can you record the view that you have chosen? Have a race with your friends, but the scene must still be recognisable and do not use an eraser.

Landscapes

A landscape painting shows an expanse of scenery as viewed from a certain place.

Composing a landscape

The artist has to consider several things before starting a landscape painting. The composition may include a horizon line, which is the point where the land and sky meet. The artist will decide what to put in the foreground, middle ground and background before sketching the large shapes in. Buildings, people or animals may be included to help give an idea of scale.

What is perspective?

Perspective is a way of drawing or painting to show distance in pictures. Artists use different tricks to show perspective. One trick is to make objects in the background smaller than those in the foreground. Another is to paint the shapes in the background in fainter tones or in less detail than those in the foreground.

▶ *Which of the tricks described above do you think the artist has used to give a sense of perspective in this landscape?*

background

middle ground

foreground

▲ *This unusual landscape, Flight in Egypt, shows a story from the Bible. The artist, Maerten Ryckaert, has put Mary and Joseph right at the front and made Mary noticeable in bright red clothes. How do the colours in the foreground compare with the tones of the background?*

3D landscape

Use what you have learned about perspective to make a three-dimensional (3D) landscape. Use a shoebox or sheet of cardboard as a base. Refer to your thumbnail sketches to help you draw the shapes of the different landscape features on card.

▶ *Tape or glue the shapes you have made into the scene to represent the foreground, middle ground and background of your view.*

◀ *Next, paint your scene. Bryonie is making the colours in the background less intense, so they look further away.*

These little sculptures will help to show the scale of my scene.

▶ *Use natural or plastic modelling clay to model some details that can be added to your landscape. Think about the size of these details and where you will place them.*

Stand back and look at your model. Does it give a sense of perspective? Perhaps you could use some of the tricks you have learned to show perspective to make scenery for the next school play or concert.

Take a trip

Is your class planning a trip to a place of interest? Perhaps you have been for a day out with your family to a beauty spot or to visit a town that is famous for its interesting buildings. The details and features found in a particular environment can help to create a sense of place.

Changing landscape

Can you find out how the landscape around your place of interest has changed over time? A local museum might have some pictures that show what life was like in the past. Compare them with the same view when you go on your visit. Perhaps more houses have been built to meet the needs of a growing population, or industry has declined in the area, leaving wasteland or derelict buildings.

▲ Bath was a popular spa town in the Georgian period, and the beautiful buildings and elegant streets designed in the 18th century have given the city a distinctive look.

◄ The landscape is changing all the time, but in some places we can still see the evidence of past civilisations. This picture shows part of Hadrian's Wall, a fortification built across northern England by the Romans nearly 2,000 years ago.

Research the area

Before your trip, research some interesting facts about the place you are visiting. What does the landscape say about the community that uses it? For instance, a farming area will have very different features from an industrial area. Collect images of contrasting locations and make a collage across two pages of your sketchbook.

On location

Once you have arrived at your location, look closely for details and features that interest you. Use your viewfinder to isolate patterns, shapes, colours or textures. Take close-up photographs of these or draw them in your sketchbook. Try to record how light reflects off the different surfaces. You can use these to inspire some further artwork, such as designing your own patterns, when you get back to school.

I am going to make an abstract painting based on my photos of these details and patterns.

Urban view

To see the work of photographic artists who are interested in urban landscapes, go to:
http://www.urbanlandscape.org.uk/

Journeys

People make all sorts of journeys during their lives – simple, short journeys to local places and longer journeys to distant places.

Maps

Maps are important for travellers because they show locations of and routes between places. Maps can help us to plan a journey and to find the way if we get lost. Some maps also use symbols to show special features such as local landmarks. Perhaps you have used a map during an orienteering exercise.

Collect examples of different maps. What do you notice about the viewpoint that each map is seen from? Is it always from above – an aerial viewpoint? Why do you think that is?

▶ *Some maps show a lot of detail, such as streets, places of interest and car parks. Others, such as a map of the world, might show countries, seas and only the major cities.*

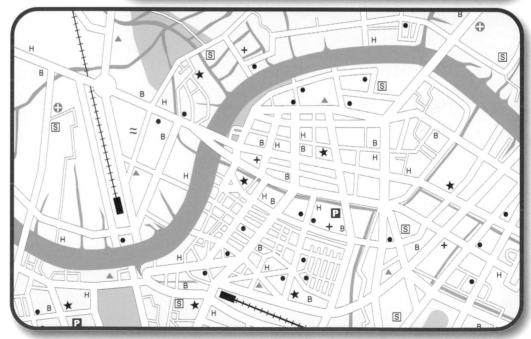

Aboriginal art

The Aboriginal people of Australia make a particular style of art that uses an aerial viewpoint so that it can be read just like a map. The artists use symbols to represent objects, places and living things that they encounter on the journey through their lives. Look at the maps that you have collected – do any of them have a key to the symbols? Aboriginal artists use a key that has been passed down through the generations and is an important part of their spiritual journey.

Imagine a journey

Use Aboriginal artwork to inspire you as you map your own imaginary journey. Where will you travel from, and where to? Create your own symbols to show important features of the environment, or animals and people that you meet along the way. Imagine that you have an

▶ *Thomas has used symbols and patterns to show the journey of a snake going to look for food in his painting inspired by Aboriginal art.*

▼ *Can you see how this snake has been painted so that we can see it from an aerial viewpoint? The Aboriginal artist has used colours that reflect the colours of the earth found in Australia.*

aerial view of the route you are going to take and plan this in your sketchbook. Once you are happy with your journey design, make a larger version using paint and pastels.

When you have finished, ask your friends if they can work out what your journey is about and what some of the symbols mean.

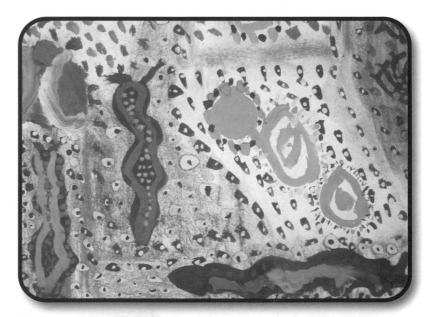

Seascapes

There is something about views of the sea and the coast that we really enjoy. Perhaps it reminds us of being on holiday or maybe we are fascinated by the power of the sea.

The sea as subject matter

There are many aspects of the sea that make it an interesting subject for artists. Can you think of some descriptive words that explain some of the different states of the sea? What effect does the weather have on the behaviour and colours of the sea?

Sea poem

Use the words you thought of to describe the sea and choose some from the word bank below to inspire an individual or class poem around the subject of the sea.

glimmer glisten shimmer calm
deep shallow silent ripple
rough tranquil stormy
splashing crystal

Collage and colours

Collect images of the sea and make a collage with them in your sketchbook. You could also make colour studies with oil pastels to investigate the huge variety of colours and tones that the sea reflects.

Paint a seascape

Try some experimental painting techniques to create effects that will help you express either a calm or rough sea. Use pudding paint (see box) with a palette knife to create a seascape on strong paper or board. Apply the paint thickly or thinly then scrape some off. Place more paint on top and try making swirls or waves to show the movement of the water. Add some white to create areas of light or foamy waves.

Recipe for pudding paint

5 cups of water, 2 cups of flour
½ cup of sugar, 3 tablespoons of salt

Mix and heat all the ingredients in a saucepan until the mixture is thick, then divide it into four bowls. Add one primary colour of poster or powder paint to three of the bowls and add white to the last bowl. Store it in the fridge when you are not using it. Mix the colours on a palette or directly on the painting itself.

Compare these two seascapes. There are obvious differences in colour and mood, but look at the composition of the pieces. Could it be the same scene in different weather conditions?

Cityscapes

It seems that more and more people are choosing to live in cities. All these people need somewhere to live and to work, and so urban areas are spreading to meet this growing need.

What is a cityscape?

Part of an artist's job is to reflect what is happening in society. Artworks that show panoramic views of the urban or built environment are called cityscapes. These artworks encourage us to think about different aspects of city life.

▲ *How does this photograph of a city skyline remind you of a traditional landscape? The photographer has used shape, colour and tone in the same way, and the sky and foreground are as important in this composition as they are in any landscape painting.*

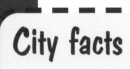

City facts

Watch the online video by artists Christian Grou and Tapio Snellman at: http://www.tate.org.uk/modern/exhibitions/globalcities/

Make written notes in your sketchbook of what you have learned from the video about cities.

City shapes

What do you notice about lines and shapes in cityscapes? Which geometric shapes do you see? Can you make thumbnail sketches of some of these, either by going into the environment itself or by looking at images of different cities?

Urban sculpture

Make a clay sculpture inspired by the built environment, using your sketches as a starting point.

▼ *Anzul is making a base for his model by rolling out clay slabs. Next, he will use slip to join the slabs at right angles to create a background.*

▶ *Anzul is modelling the clay by cutting, rolling and pulling it into shapes. He is adding texture by pressing into the surface before fixing the separate pieces together using slip.*

I'm marking a river on my model.

▼ *The final sculpture was dried, fired in the kiln and glazed.*

Cloudscapes

How often do you look up into the sky? You may think of clouds as white, fluffy cotton wool balls on a sheet of blue, but the reality is much more interesting and varied. Skies are changing all the time and the colours in clouds can be very dramatic and bright.

True or false?

Perhaps you have heard this proverb: 'Red sky at night, shepherd's delight. Red sky at morning, shepherd's warning.'

Keep a cloud diary in which you could sketch, photograph or note down the cloud shapes, colours and patterns that you observe over a period of time.

Do you think that the message in the proverb is true?

Moody skies

Clouds and skies are an important feature of landscape painting and contribute to the way that we read the whole scene. They can add to the mood in the work and provide a sense of scale and perspective.

▲ *Have you ever seen colours such as orange, pink and purple in a sunset or at dawn?*

Constable's clouds

The artist John Constable is well known for his paintings of English landscapes, but the clouds and skies in Constable's work are an essential part of how he sets the scene. They show the changing light and atmosphere of the view, which helps the viewer to gain a sense of place.

Constable loved to work directly from nature in the open air of the countryside and this allowed him to develop a free and expressive way of using paint.

▲ *The clouds in this landscape by John Constable seem to be the main focus of the painting as they take up almost two-thirds of the picture. How do you think this adds to the atmosphere of the scene?*

Painting the skies

Use your cloud diary to inspire some paintings of skies. Use primary colours and white poster paint to mix all the colours that you will need. Challenge yourself to mix a variety of greys without using any black.

Make a display with the finished work. How many ways did you find to show the beauty of our changing skies?

▶ *The young artist who produced this painting used large brushes and tried to be free and expressive with the paint, just like John Constable.*

Around the world

Looking at paintings and photographs of different places from around the world can help us to understand what landscapes are like in other countries and compare them to our own.

Weather and climate

Weather conditions and climate will determine what the colours and textures in the natural world are like in different environments. Looking at paintings of different places can help us to imagine what they are like – and what it might be like to live there.

▲ This painting, Matamoe, is by Paul Gauguin and was painted in 1892, a year after he moved to Polynesia. What do you imagine the temperature might be like in this beautiful place? What clues have you used to help you work that out?

◀ Compare this icy scene painted by Pieter Bruegel to the island paradise above. Make a list of all the differences that you can find. Can you spot any similarities between the two views?

Jungle fever

The self-taught artist Henri Rousseau was fascinated with jungle environments. Very surprisingly, Rousseau's paintings of magical and exotic jungle scenes were entirely from his own imagination inspired by visits to the botanical gardens and the zoo in Paris, where he lived. The animals were often copied from pictures in books and other paintings.

▶ *This painting by Rousseau is called* The Merry Jesters. *Do you think that these monkeys look merry (happy) and that their behaviour is natural? The monkeys are holding a backscratcher and a milk bottle. How do you think these objects could have got into the scene?*

Install your own jungle

Create your own jungle environment in a corner of the classroom. Use recycled materials, sticks and paper of different textures and colours. Paint paper or fabric to create as many shades of green as you can and then cut, tear, plait or curl it to make leaves of different shapes and sizes.

Mixed-media painting

Investigate how climate change is affecting our world by looking at the photographs of Yann Arthus-Bertrand: http://www.wecommunic8.com/earthfromtheair/

Make a painting inspired by the photographs using a wide variety of media. For example, you might mix sand or earth into paint to represent dried riverbeds or mix flour with water to show melting icecaps.

Viewpoints

When we watch a film or television show, we might not take too much notice of the location where the action is taking place. This could be because we find the actors or the storyline more interesting. However, the scene that surrounds the action sets the atmosphere and mood, so it is an essential part of creating dramatic effects.

Choosing viewpoints

Viewing a scene from an unexpected angle can make an image more interesting and a photographer can move his or her body into a certain position in order to take a particular shot.

Christine works as a camera operator for films and television. She has brought her camera along to school to show the children how to look for unusual viewpoints by using the camera's viewfinder.

▲ *Special lighting is often used to create a certain mood. Shadows and specially angled lights can create a sense of mystery and anticipation.*

▶ *Christine is showing Hannah and Leon how placing a camera on a tripod allows time for the photographer to find a good composition and keeps the camera very still while the picture is being taken.*

A sense of drama

Use a digital camera or video recorder to take some dramatic photographs or make a short film using light and shadows to create a sense of emotion and atmosphere. Try using interesting views by looking down or up at your subject, around, through and underneath objects, or by looking at images reflected in different surfaces.

Print the photographs out or watch the video in colour and in black and white. Which do you consider to be more successful?

Painted viewpoints

The American artist Edward Hopper painted quiet, lonely scenes with no or very few people in them. Hopper adds to the sense of unease in his paintings by using shadowy tones. Look at the viewpoints from which Hopper chose to paint his scenes at: http://www.ibiblio.org/wm/paint/auth/hopper/

Emotions

Go to different windows around the school and sketch the views you see through them. You might be looking out or looking in. What emotions do the different views make you feel? Maybe you feel calm when you look into a quiet area or excited if you can see sports being played in the gym. Can you use colours in your sketches to represent these emotions?

◀ *Hopper has chosen to capture this view of a man at a petrol station from a slightly raised position. This angle adds to the sense of strangeness and loneliness about the scene, as if we are spying on the man. The dark woods in the background also add to the sense of mystery.*

Architecture

Individual buildings, or structures, can instantly give us a sense of place, particularly if they are very famous. Examples might be the Eiffel Tower in Paris or the Statue of Liberty in New York. These unique buildings become part of the identity of a country or city and this makes them very important.

Ancient structures

The buildings that still remain from ancient civilisations reveal a great deal about the people who lived in them, or used them for other reasons, such as worship. The Colosseum in Rome began to be built in the year 70 AD and was completed ten years later. It is an amphitheatre, a building that was used for public games and contests between gladiators.

Where in the world?

Which of these buildings do you recognise? Can you name which country and city each of them is in?

◀ *Look at the ruined state of the Colosseum today. This is due to earthquake damage and because people have taken the stones over the years. What do you think would happen to buildings if people continued to take pieces from them?*

Architects

An architect has to be a combination of artist, scientist and mathematician – being able to design buildings means having skills in all these areas. An architect's measurements need to be exact, so that buildings are constructed accurately and are safe for people to live and work in.

Towering above

Have a competition with your friends to see who can build the highest tower, by taping tight newspaper rolls together. How will you make sure that your tower balances and doesn't fall over? Will it be symmetrical? You might have to place the tubes of paper at diagonal angles and tape them firmly into place.

▶ *Turn your structure into a sculpture by adding coloured tissue paper or cellophane to fill in the gaps and display it lit with fairy lights.*

Architecture online

Test your knowledge of structures and materials and find out about an artist who makes gingerbread houses at: http://www.archkidecture.org/

Land Art and public art

Land Art, or environmental art, is where the artist has used the land itself to create the artwork. This differs from 'public art', where a work – for instance a sculpture – is placed either in the landscape or in a certain public area.

Earthy materials

Land Art is sometimes called Earth Art, or Earthworks, and these names give us a clue about the media that the artists use.

▲ Can you think of any more materials that Land artists might use?

Shapes in nature

The Land Art movement began in the 1960s and 70s, as some artists wanted to work with nature to break away from the limits set by gallery spaces. One of the first and most famous pieces of Land Art is *Spiral Jetty* by Robert Smithson. It was inspired by the Great Serpent Mound, which is thought to be an ancient effigy site in Ohio, USA, made by the Fort Ancient Indians. Look at *Spiral Jetty* online at: http://www.robertsmithson.com/earthworks/spiral_jetty.htm

▲ Look carefully at the curved shapes looping up and down the Great Serpent Mound. If the snake were stretched out to full length, it would be over 365 metres long.

Sculpting the land

Contemporary artist Richard Long makes his work by walking in the landscape, and his sculptures develop as his footprints make an impression on the ground. Have you ever walked across a damp or frosty lawn and noticed the trail of flattened grass that you leave behind? Richard Long would record this by photographing it, or mapping the journey of the area that he has covered. See examples at: http://www.richardlong.org/sculptures/sculptures.html

Sculpture design

Design a piece of public art for your school grounds. Take photographs of some areas that you might use within the school grounds and print one out when you have decided on a place for your sculpture. Think carefully about the materials you would like to use. Perhaps you could use natural materials like the Land artists.

Make sketches to work out your idea before drawing the final design directly on to your print of the area. Does your sculpture need

▲ Can you see a path here that has been worn by people walking along? Do you think that this could be considered a 'drawing in the land'?

changing or developing in any way? Show the designs to your headteacher, and perhaps he or she will choose one that your class could make collaboratively, to be placed in the school grounds.

Glossary

abstract   describes artwork that is not obviously a picture of something.

aerial viewpoint   a view from the air.

aperture   an opening or gap.

architect   a person who designs buildings.

atmosphere   a mood or tone that can be created.

civilisation   a particular society that works well due to its own set of rules. We usually think of a civilisation as having developed to an advanced stage.

climate   the average weather of a place over a period of time.

climate change   changes in the climate of the Earth as a whole, including rising temperatures, which is sometimes called global warming.

collaboratively   together with other people.

collage   an artwork made by sticking images or fabrics on to a flat surface.

composition   the arrangement of different elements to create a whole piece of artwork.

contemporary   of the same time or period. In this context it means the present day.

derelict   run down or abandoned.

dramatic effects   the addition of lighting or sound to a staged drama in order to create a particular mood.

effigy   a rough representation of a person or animal.

expressive   showing meaning or feeling, very clearly.

Fort Ancient Indians   Native Americans who lived around Ohio, USA, from 1000 to 1650 AD. They are known for building mounds, especially burial mounds.

found objects   existing objects.

geometric   relating to geometry. Geometry is the area of mathematics that deals with lines, angles and shapes.

Georgian   the period of British history from 1714 to 1830 covering the reigns of George I, II, III and IV.

illustrate	to add pictures to a text.
intense	strong or very extreme.
key	a list of words to explain pictorial symbols.
kiln	a very hot oven that is specially designed for baking pottery.
landscape	a picture showing natural scenery or countryside.
medium	(plural **media**) a particular material or technique used by an artist.
oil pastel	a medium that has the texture of a wax crayon, but which allows colours to be blended more easily, especially when a little oil is added.
orienteering	a sport that involves people finding their way across country using a map and compass.
revolutionary	completely new or ground-breaking.
rural	characteristic of the countryside.
scale	relative size.
sketchbook	a plain paged book an artist uses to keep visual information to use another time. A sketchbook can be used for note taking, memory jogging, to solve problems or experiment with ideas and techniques.
slab	a thick slice.
slip	clay that has been dissolved in water so that it can be used as a glue to join two pieces of clay together.

spiritual journey	the search for truth and meaning in life.
symbol	an image of one thing standing for another thing, for example a heart shape is used to mean 'love'.
texture	the feel of a surface.
three-dimensional	having height, width and depth.
thumbnail sketch	a small, quick sketch, often made in preparation for a larger work.
tone	the lightness, darkness or quality of colour.
tripod	a three-legged support for a camera.
urban	characteristic of city life.
viewfinder	a device for isolating a small area from a larger view.
viewpoint	a particular standpoint from which something is seen.
visualise	to imagine or think of images in your mind.

For teachers and parents

This book is designed to cover the learning objectives of the QCA Schemes of Work for Art and Design in KS2. Its aim is to provide imaginative and contemporary ways of working with the schemes. Specifically it covers Unit 6C A Sense of Place, but essential elements of Unit 3C Can we change places?, 4A Viewpoints and 4C Journeys are also included.

Children might have already experienced Units 1A What is sculpture? and 2C Can buildings speak?

The ideas and activities are designed to act as starting points for deeper investigation and, in line with the programmes of study, it should be remembered that all the activities take place within the process of:

- Exploring and developing ideas.
- Investigating and making art, craft and design.
- Evaluating and developing work.
- Developing knowledge and understanding.

SUGGESTED FURTHER ACTIVITIES

Pages 4 - 5 The local environment
An alternative to a stapled or stitched book for the activity would be a concertina book that shows sketches and items from the journey in sequence.

Set up an exhibition with all the discoveries, posters and brochures made by the children, and invite members of your school community to come and visit. Leave some pencils and paper for visitors to write comments or tell stories of their own experiences of the local environment.

Pages 6 - 7 Sketching the environment
When asking children to make these quick sketches, it can be useful to simplify the task by encouraging them to look at shapes only, or horizontal and vertical lines only. They might make tonal or colour sketches in the same way, by choosing the darkest and lightest areas to draw, or using oil pastels to make patches of colour. The important thing is that the sketch acts as a reminder of the place, not a photographic-style representation.

Build on the understanding of a sensory approach from the previous pages by using Turner's work as a starting point for an investigation into

a visual expression of sensations. Sprinkle powder paint or Brusho granules on to wet paper to create paint effects. When the paper is dry, draw on to it with pencil or charcoal.

Pages 8 - 9 Landscapes
Download the teachers' pack for 'Picture of Britain', which includes images and related ideas for activities, from: http://www.tate.org.uk/learning/apictureofbritain/teacherspacks/apictureofbritain.pdf

Look at the spatial illusions created by contemporary artist Matthias Weischer at: http://www.saatchi-gallery.co.uk/artists/matthias_weischer.htm and at the perspective in this painting by American artist Inka Essenhigh: http://www.saatchi-gallery.co.uk/artists/artpages/essenhigh_Blue_Wave.htm

Pages 10 - 11 Take a trip
On your visit, encourage the children to make critical judgments about the place of interest. For instance, you could ask them which they consider to be the most beautiful building or what permanent fixture they would remove to improve the environment?

Encourage the children to look at buildings reflected in shop windows or car bumpers to see how they distort and look as if they could not remain standing. Back in class, ask the children to use these ideas to draw a building that could not actually be built.

Pages 12 - 13 Journeys
Link a project such as the one described here with literacy, and ask the children to write about their journey in an imaginative way.

There is information about Aboriginal culture and a whole section on the art, iconography and artists on these two websites: http://aboriginalart.com.au/ and http://www.aboriginalartonline.com/culture/symbols.php

Challenge the children to think about all the different uses we have for map reading in everyday life and in work situations. Schools can register for free online mapping services and resources at: http://www.infomapper.com

Pages 14 - 15 Seascapes
Encourage the children to experiment with materials to create different effects: oil pastels can be used quite thickly and colours layered over

one another to create a choppy sea effect. They can also be blended together by adding a little cooking oil, for a smooth calm sea.

At http://blog.tate.org.uk/tate-tales/?p=4 children can write their own story in response to the painting *Space and Matter* by Sandra Blow.

Pages 16 - 17 Cityscapes
Download the teachers' notes for Global Cities at: http://www.tate.org.uk /modern/exhibitions/globalcities/pdf/global_cities_teachers_pack.pdf

Use clay to create a large-scale imagined city that all the children can contribute to. Allow plenty of clay and let the children use free modelling techniques, such as boring holes through, gouging out clay with clay tools to show doors and windows, building tall towers and twisting clay to make unusual shapes before air drying the sculpture. Look at the work of Antoni Gaudi for inspiration: http://www.greatbuildings.com/architects/ Antonio_Gaudi.html

Children can build their own imaginary city at: http://www.tate.org.uk/kids/city/

Pages 18 - 19 Cloudscapes
Wait for a day when there are clouds in the sky and take your class outside. Ask them to lie down in the play area and encourage them to look for imaginative shapes in the clouds. How quickly are the shapes changing? Can they see them metamorphosing into something new?

Use the images from this website on the whiteboard as a discussion point: http://www.skyscapes.org.uk/index.html

The painting shown is *Old Sarum*. Some of Constable's oil sketches of skies and clouds can be viewed at:http://www.vam.ac.uk/collections/ paintings/galleries/display/constable_oil/index.html

Pages 20 - 21 Around the world
The picture by Pieter Bruegel the Elder is *Hunters in the Snow*. Link an art project on weather with Unit 7 from the QCA Geography Scheme of Work, Weather Around the World. You could look at examples of art or photographs that show extreme conditions.

Children could investigate endangered animals and then create animal sculptures using papier mâché or Modroc/plaster bandage to display within their jungle environment.

The David Shepherd Foundation runs an art competition each year around the theme of wild and endangered animals: http://www.davidshepherd.org/

Pages 22 - 23 Viewpoints
Ask the children to look around the school and think about the shapes that are created by seeing something from a different perspective. The QCA scheme 'Viewpoints' suggests using photographs taken from the viewpoints that you find to develop a dream sequence. You might also use your photographs or sketches as starting points for writing some poetry around this theme.

The Hopper painting shown is *Gas*. Children could find images in newspapers and magazines that show objects or people photographed from unusual angles. Look at *Breakfast* by Alexander Rodchenko on: http://www.tate.org.uk/valueart/value/working/artworks/ everydaylife.htm

Pages 24 - 25 Architecture
The buildings shown are: Saint Basil's Cathedral, Moscow, Russia (top left); Houses of Parliament, London, UK (top right); Opera House, Sydney, Australia (centre left); Empire State Building, New York, USA (centre right); Leaning Tower of Pisa, Italy (bottom left); Taj Mahal, Agra, India (bottom right).

Develop a cross-curricular art and maths project to explore geometry, shape and space. Science and design and technology can also be part of an investigation into how structures are made. Try joining uncooked spaghetti with marshmallows to see who can build the tallest tower.

See more examples of structures made by children on this Canadian website: http://www.yesmag.ca/projects/geodesic.html

Pages 26 - 27 Land Art and public art
Explore environmental themes and concerns by linking an art project with geography or citizenship.

Type 'environmental art' into the search facility on the Princeton University website for lots of lesson plans and further related weblinks at: http://www.princetonol.com/groups/iad/

The UK schools charity, Learning through Landscapes, gives advice on how to develop school grounds in ways that will support children's learning: http://www.ltl.org.uk/

For images of environmental and Land Art by contemporary artists, go to: http://www.the-artists.org/movement/Land__Environmental.html

Index